THE GIANT BOOK OF 'HOW-TO' LISTS FOR THE NEW DAD

MUMS
IN THE
KNOW

First Edition

To Our Beloved Husbands:
Thank you for being the inspiration behind this book.
Even though you wish you weren't.

LIST #ONE:
10 THINGS TO EXPECT WHILST SHE IS EXPECTING

Your life changes the moment your partner discovers she is pregnant. Here are some of the things you will instantly be confronted with:

1. Random people coming up to your partner to touch her stomach and inquire about the pregnancy.

2. The same random people telling you what you are having, whether or not you wanted to know.

3. Anyone who has a child bombarding you with numerous tips and advice on how to raise your unborn offspring.

4. Serious mood swings by your partner. They can be extreme, without warning, and completely irrational. They are normal and will pass.

5. Your partner's energy levels and spirits dropping considerably. You will have to do a lot more around the house and pay special attention to your lady.

6. People suddenly regarding you as a grown-up, and making you feel guilty for having a drunken night out with the boys. Or any night with the boys.

7. Your partner being elevated to celebrity status, with people holding doors open and giving up seats for her.

8. A full range of feelings flowing through you: from excitement to mortal fear. For a complete list of emotions you will experience, refer to **LIST #SIXTEEN**.

9. Your partner's inability to walk up a flight of stairs without stopping 3 times.

10. In later pregnancy, your partner's inability to get a good night's sleep and her waking you up several times through the night to tell you so.

LIST #TWO:
9 WAYS TO DESTROY THE PERFECT BABYMOON

Your babymoon is the last chance you will get to travel as a couple, enjoy a candlelight dinner at leisure, get dressed without anyone climbing into your cupboard and generally be alone and harmonious with each other. Don't screw it up by doing any of the following:

1. Picking a destination that is all about the sights so that you return to your room at night exhausted and monumented-out.

2. Booking pre-planned tours that don't allow any time off or flexibility.

3. Making it a "roughing-it" trip where you are sleeping in a tent and hunting for your dinner.

4. Taking her to Vegas for a wild weekend of drinking and gambling.

5. Inviting your parents.

6. Driving through deserted country in which bathrooms are five hours apart.

7. Making it a whirlwind "around the world" trip because you fear you won't be able to travel again till the kid is in college.

8. Being more than 15 miles away from your closest hospital or emergency room.

9. Going to a Club Med, Disneyworld or other child-infested resort (you will be spending the next 15 odd years of your life at these places so maybe try one of those institutions that tactfully say "We do not cater to children under 12 years").

LIST #THREE:
8 SIGNS YOUR WIFE NEEDS A NEW OB/GYN

Your partner will be depending on her OB/GYN to take her through the pregnancy. Look out for these signs that might indicate she's picked the wrong one:

1. He doesn't return your calls within four hours.

2. He is not able to answer all your questions and keeps referring to Google for the answers.

3. He is not able to make her feel at ease and alleviate most of her concerns, if not all.

4. He either gives too much data or not enough data.

5. He makes jokes when you come in with serious fears and questions.

6. He acts as if childbirth is the most banal process in the world and blatantly disregards that fact that though this is his hundredth delivery, it's your first.

7. He insists on scheduling a cesarean so that your childbirth does not interfere with golf/vacation plans.

8. Your partner is doing her nails, hair and bikini line every time she goes to see him.

LIST #FOUR:
9 ESSENTIALS FOR BABY'S FIRST MONTH

Especially since your partner is going to get carried away and buy tons of unnecessary stuff, make sure you have the basics covered:

1. Car seat - There are many options out there so do your research. Many hospitals won't let you leave if you don't have a car seat properly installed so be sure to have it organized before your discharge date.

2. Stroller - Once again, there are many options so try to go into a baby store and test them out. Strollers vary greatly based on size, shape, cost and storage, so depending on your needs, get a store assistant to help you make the right decision.

3. Change table - You will be changing your child's diaper about 10 times a day, so a change table at is a worthwhile investment to protect your back and store things so that you can reach for them with one hand (while holding down your squirming baby)

4. Bassinet/crib - Many parents have their newborns in their rooms in a bassinet for the first few months. If you are looking at buying only the bare essentials, you can always just place her into the cot first without buying a bassinet.

5. Swaddles - Swaddles emulate the feeling in the womb and prevent the baby from waking herself up with jerking limbs in the middle of the night. You will use them for the first few months of the baby's life and depending on weather conditions where you live can choose between muslin, cotton, fleece, jersey or some combination.

6. Diapers - For a newborn, you will be changing diapers 8-10 times a day. Depending on the size of your baby, you may skip "newborn" sizes altogether, so don't buy too many until the baby is actually born.

7. Clothes - Newborn babies grow incredibly fast, so resist the urge to buy them heaps of expensive clothes. It is best to have enough clothes to last a month factoring in at least two changes a day. Baby onesies are the best for this age, and come in different lengths and styles suitable for varied weather conditions.

8. Feeding time - If your partner chooses to breastfeed, it will certainly make feeding time less preparation. If you are going to bottle feed, you will need about six 4- to 5-ounce bottles, a sterilizer, a bottlebrush and a sterilizer.

9. Bath time - You will need a baby bath or seat, a baby wash and a moisturizer. Avoid anything with strong fragrances and scents as the baby may be allergic to them. A gentle wash cloth is also advised to wash the baby's face.

Everybody wants a piece of the eager new parent with the unlimited credit card. Save your moolah by skipping these non value-add items below:

1. Baby monitor with sensors - These overpriced pieces of equipment promise to alert you within 20 seconds if your baby stops breathing. If your baby is not breathing for 20 seconds, there is nothing you can do. Plus the frequent false alarms on these things will make you paranoid.

2. The bath bucket -These seem like a great idea for the space conscious, however they are completely impractical. It is virtually impossible to reach inside the bucket to wash your baby in one of these as babies are often so tightly snug in it. If they are not snug yet, then they will be in no time, and the bath bucket will soon be an expensive accompaniment to your mop.

3. Stretch mark creams - Stretch marks are genetic, so even a $1000 cream won't work. If your partner is unlucky enough to get stretch marks, unfortunately only time will make them go away. Sad, but true.

4. Mobiles - Placing a mobile over your baby's sleeping place can actually prevent her from falling asleep as it is visual stimulation. Plus, many mobiles you see in stores are designed for the adult's viewing pleasure, not the baby's: they are only cute when viewed from the side, not from the bottom!

5. Baby Einstein videos and CDs - While DVDs and cds are very popular with little kids, don't pay the extra for the "Baby Einstein" brand. Disney themselves put out a release stating that these do not accelerate children's development as previously claimed, and in some countries, they are $20/pop. Further, as there are studies that show that television watching is not recommended for babies under the age of 2, you are much better off buying your baby a picture book.

6. Overpriced Diaper Bags - You need a diaper bag, but not a designer, expensive one. Something durable with multiple pockets, a zipper and that is waterproof will do the trick.

7. Breastfeeding bracelets - Ok, granted they are only a couple of dollars but your partner really doesn't need a plastic strap to remind her

which breast to feed from. If you want to decorate her wrists, buy her a tennis bracelet.

8. Excessive toys - You can spend $500 on a single toy when your baby is under 3 years old, and he wouldn't care less. When it comes to toys, keep it simple. Kids have amazing imaginations, and don't need super built-up, flashing, whizzing, popping gadgets. Check out **LIST #FORTY-FOUR** for the most popular toys with kids that won't cost you much at all.

9. Breastfeeding pillow - Breastfeeding pillows are meant to provide support to both mother and baby whilst breastfeeding. However using large pillows can easily recreate what this achieves and saves you the $50 you would otherwise shell out.

LIST #SIX:
14 MUST-HAVES FOR YOUR BATHROOM CABINET

Move over hair products and anti-aging cream, the baby meds are here!

1. Panadol/Tylenol (acetaminophen) for all-purpose pains and symptoms

2. Anti-inflammatory (ibuprofen) for teething pains, over-night fevers

3. Colic relief/gripe water for stomach discomfort

4. Saline spray and aspirator for nasal congestion

5. Karvol or baby Vicks for nasal congestion

6. Teething gel

7. Antiseptic cream for small cuts and scratches

8. Antiseptic wash

9. Bandages

10. Syringes (3-5mls)

11. Vaseline or diaper rash cream for nappy rash

12. Ice pack for little bumps and bruises

13. Thermometer

14. Cotton buds and balls

LIST #SEVEN:
THE BREAKDOWN OF COSTS FOR BABY'S 1ST YEAR

Baby equipment can run from your basic Honda to a built-up Aston Martin. How much you can afford to spend is up to you. Here's a rough idea of what you're up against:

1. Car seat - These run anywhere from $50 to $300. Infant car seats are backwards-facing and toddler car seats are forwards-facing although you can buy some that convert. Not something to skimp on because safety must be your primary concern. That being said, middle of the range is probably a good bet.

2. Crib - Cribs can range from $200 to $1500. The most important considerations should be safety, stability and having a drop-door that opens with one hand and snaps shut. One that converts into a toddler bed will buy you 6 months or so more before you need to upgrade.

3. Bassinet - Your baby may sleep in a bassinet for the first 4-6 months. Bassinets range from $75 to $300.

4. Stroller - Can go from $100 to $1000, with interchangeable seats and various accessories. Look for something light, sturdy and portable. Having a bassinet for a newborn baby is a plus so they can sleep flat while you are off running errands or venture out to your neighbourhood trattoria for dinner. That being said, many parents swap out their expensive, bulky travel systems for a much more manageable (and cheaper) Maclaren or such. Do your research and decide which works for you.

5. Changing table - Definitely a worthwhile investment if you don't want to end up stooping over for the first 2-3 years of the baby's life. Changing tables run from $100 to $500 and come with various options for drawers, shelves, etc. Ensure that you can put diapers, wipes, creams and a toy (for entertainment) on it and that is has a strap to keep the baby secure.

6. High Chair - High chairs have a weight limit so it is up to you to figure out the trade-off between how long you can use them and how much to spend. Some come with various seating positions and other fancy options. Range is between $50 and $300.

7. Baby Carrier - Between $50 and $200. Some baby carriers have been in the news lately for suffocating and killing babies so better to stick with the known brands.

8. Clothes - Your baby will grow out of clothes faster than you go through a beer and will spit up or poop on most of them, so avoid shopping at Baby Dior for everyday wear. Multi-packs of onesies and footie sleepwear should do it for the first few months, along with a ton of socks.

9. Diapers/Wipes/Toiletries - Diapers in bulk (which is totally worth buying) cost about 0.50cents/diaper. You will be using about 10/day for the first three months and then about 6/day.

10. Formula - Varies by brand. Generic brands cost about $30 for 24 ounces, while more specialized formulas for lactose intolerance and reflux symptoms are more expensive.

11. Babysitters - While this is not something you may use if you choose to stay home for the first fifteen years of your baby's life or if you have help or family close by, but for most other people babysitters are an inevitable cost of having a baby. Babysitters that are qualified to look after a new baby charge $20-$30/hour and should have police clearances, ID cards and references available.

12. Toys - Don't waste your money; people will give you toys for gifts plus everything you really need is on LIST #FORTY-FOUR.

LIST #EIGHT:
10 BEST BABY PRODUCTS ON THE MARKET

You can actually go crazy (and broke!) with all the stuff that is available for babies. Here's our list of must-have products to help you navigate the barrage:

1. A baby carrier – Aside from the fact that "carrying your baby" is a fashion statement, it's also a great way to take the baby around while having both hands free. Baby carriers are also helpful when traveling or in tight spaces where strollers are harder to take along.

2. Diaper bin - Let's face it, babies come with a lot of shit. Diaper bins help you contain it and seal off the odor.

3. A swaddle – Wrapping may become the bane of your existence if your baby is a mini Harry Houdini and manages to get himself out of even the tightest and most complicated hold. This is where a good swaddle comes in handy so that your baby will stay tightly and neatly wrapped and you don't need to learn origami in the process.

4. A portable high chair - If you're a parent on-the-go, invest in a portable high chair that is usually a kind of sling that wraps a baby and straps him to a chair. They usually roll up into a pouch and are easy to wash and take anywhere.

5. A play mat - These can be a savior and can entertain your baby for a long time. The play mat provides visual stimulation, development of fine motor skills and muscle development. Every baby needs a good play mat, if at least for a change of scene!

6. A bath seat - Bath seats are great as it means you can have 2 free hands to wash your baby. It also creates a calm and relaxed bath time for your baby as it provides comfortable support and has an adjustable backrest. For those of you with limited storage, it folds flat and is easy to travel with as well.

7. An electrical or microwave sterilizer - These are especially invaluable if you are bottle feeding your child. Of course, you could easily boil whatever item you need to sterilize, but it is much quicker and there are fewer items to clean with an electrical or microwave sterilizer. It's all done with a flick of a switch!

8. A portacot - If you plan on doing a bit of travel, even for weekends, these are great. Babies pick up on new smells and surroundings, and will settle easier if you can eliminate unfamiliar things. Be sure to pack your own bed sheets as well.

9. An exersaucer - This toy will save your life. Ok, that may be a little extreme, but it will actually give you a life. The exersaucer is an activity center for a baby who is at least 6 months old. It is the perfect toy for when you want to have a quick shower, make a phone call or even read the paper. Babies stand (or sit) in the exersaucer and play with the toys that surround them. The real beauty of this toy is that it gives you the comfort of knowing that your child will be in the same place when you turn around (priceless!).

10. Toilet seat clasp - Babies have a knack for finding the most unpleasant places in the house. Putting a clasp on your toilet seat will ensure that little fingers won't make their way into the toilet bowl to explore its contents, or splatter them around the room.

LIST #NINE:
10 NAMES GUARANTEED TO GET HIM/HER TORTURED
AT SCHOOL

Many parents believe that the baby's name is about them, not about the child. Pay attention to these faux-pas below to ensure that your child's name doesn't screw them for life:

1. Anything that rhymes with smelly (Nelly), ugly (Dudley) or fat (Pat).

2. Middle names that will leave them with initials like D.O.G. or S.T.D.

3. Undesirable abbreviated nicknames e.g. Richard becoming Dick.

4. Words that turn obscene with the addition of a prefix such as "Master Bate" or "Miss Conception".

5. Anything that rhymes with or sounds like a part of the human anatomy such as Dolores, Eunice or Uranus.

6. 3 or more syllable names particularly if you are an ethnic minority in a country.

7. Names that were popular in Greek mythology or in past centuries like "Prudence" or "Hercules" (unless of course, you are Greek or from the last century).

8. Naming the baby after the place or position in which he was conceived: "Truck", "Rock" or "Missionary".

9. Names that are self-proclaimed titles such as "Prince", "Duke" or "God".

10. After fruits or vegetables or produce in general, unless you are a celebrity, or a plant.

DELIVERY AND THE BIRTH

LIST #TEN:
THE ESSENTIAL WEEK-OF-LABOR TO-DO LIST

You've seen it in the movies, and yes, labor is MANIC! Save yourself the stress and be prepared:

1. The baby can come ANYTIME. Keep your phone on, charged and on your person ALWAYS.

2. Have the crib, diapers, car seat, and clothes ready. Refer to **LIST #FOUR** for everything you will need.

3. Make sure there is gas in the car. This seems obvious, but you'd be amazed at how many husbands spend a year on the couch because of it.

4. Do not travel from six weeks before your due date; babies have a mind of their own and have a knack for showing up when least convenient.

5. Practice driving to the hospital so you know you can get there in less than optimal conditions (sleep-deprivation, rain, snow, screaming partner, etc.).

6. Alert your office that if they don't hear from you for 12 hours, it's because the baby has arrived. This saves you the hassle of having to excuse yourself from a conference call while holding up your partner's legs during labor.

7. Make sure you have a few meals frozen away for the first few days after you return if there is no relative or friend helping you out.

8. Have a bag packed for the hospital all ready to go. Refer to the **LIST #ELEVEN** for its contents.

9. Rest up as much as you can.

10. Go out for a nice dinner and a movie, just the two of you. Chances are it will probably be a while before you get to do this again.

LIST #ELEVEN:
EVERYTHING YOU NEED IN YOUR HOSPITAL BAG
(AND YOUR PARTNER'S)

If you think it's a cliché to have your hospital bag packed, think again. When your partner goes into labor, the last thing you will want to do is be looking for is your toothbrush.

1. 2 sets of pajamas

2. Clothes to take your baby home in plus a blanket and a hat

3. Camera - If you want to remain married, make sure you ask her permission first before you take ANY photos

4. Candy - Labor can go on for a several hours and your partner will need some sugar for sustenance

5. Music for ambiance for labor

6. Heat packs for pain relief

7. Maternity pads because she'll be bleeding for a while

8. Breast pads for when her milk comes in

9. 2 nursing bras

10. Her toiletries (including some make up so she will look like a human being in the photos and for visitors)

11. Champagne

12. A smile and an open mind for the labor

LIST #TWELVE:
10 WAYS TO COMFORT HER IN THE LABOR ROOM

There's a reason it's called labor: it's the most discomfort your partner will ever experience, and you can play a big role in alleviating some of the pain by doing the following:

1. Carry an extra pair of socks – it can get really cold in the labor room.

2. Carry a portable fan – it can get really hot in the labor room.

3. Be the Gatekeeper - The last thing your partner will want is to answer frantic calls/texts from her or your family asking how many centimeters she is dilated. Take over her phone, seal the doors, and tell everyone you'll call them when the baby is ready to go to college.

4. Sign off from your work completely. Your partner needs to know you are 100% hers.

5. Establish a rapport with the doctor and midwife/nurse before things get into full swing so that your partner knows that you will be able to collaborate with them to make the best decisions in the event that she can't.

6. Promise her that you will only take pictures in which she looks radiant, rested and thin.

7. Promise her that you will not videotape any part of the process in which she is grunting, screaming or oozing bodily fluids.

8. Resist the urge to disagree with anything she says. It may be detrimental to her health and yours.

9. Have your steady stash of massage oils, heat packs, granola bars and candles for whatever will work with her mood, which will change every 5 minutes (and that is perfectly acceptable).

10. Keep your emotions to yourself. Whatever you are feeling, remember, it doesn't compare.

LIST #THIRTEEN:
8 WAYS TO BE USEFUL DURING LABOR

Labor can last anywhere from two hours to two days and that's a long time to be irrelevant. Here are some tips to avoid just that:

1. Try making your partner as comfortable as possible (refer to **LIST #TWELVE**).

2. Resist the temptation to offer advice on what YOU think is best for her during labor. Just be supportive and acknowledge that you have no idea what she is going through but she's a goddess for doing it.

3. Respond with "Yes Dear" to her every request. Remember, your partner is not in a rational mental state while in labor, so in the interest of not getting thrown out of the room or the marriage, try to appease her. This also applies to the demands that are completely unrealistic, unreasonable and unachievable.

4. Put on a hot bath for her with her favorite scents and candles (unless her waters have already broken, in which case offer a massage) to relax her muscles and hopefully speed up the process of labor. A bath can also relieve some of the pain.

5. Do not get offended by any insults she hurls at you. You are after all, responsible for putting her in this position.

6. Understand that any birthing plans you and your partner may have made pre-labor may be tossed out the window at this time. Just go with the flow: if she wants you out of the room, run, and if she wants you holding her legs open, bear the weight with a smile.

7. Get out of the way in a hurry if the medical team needs to get in for emergency procedures. Be present and watch your partner for cues to see if she wants you to intervene.

8. DO NOT PASS OUT. "Dad Down" syndrome will haunt you for the rest of your life. If you think you won't be able to handle it, be honest with your partner and excuse yourself from the delivery room. It's better than the mid-wife having to abandon your partner mid-contraction to resuscitate you.

LIST #FOURTEEN:
7 WAYS TO COMFORT YOURSELF POST-DELIVERY

You might be in shock after the birth of your first child. Here are a few tips that can help restore mental order:

1. Cry - What you have just gone though is massive. It's the biggest thing you will experience in your life and it may hit you all at once. Cry tears of joy, relief, exhaustion and fear, if that's what's coming to you.

2. Tell Your Partner You Love Her - It will help you to release all that emotion and expressing your love to your partner will reinforce that you made this miracle together.

3. Hug Your Parents - It's a moment for you to share with those you love and your parents will understand the significance of this milestone in your life. Plus, they will probably know that you are scared shitless and be able to offer some comfort.

4. Start a Website - Some men just need something to do to cope. Upload all your pictures and videos to a site/blog for the world to see (See **LIST #TWELVE** for picture protocols during delivery).

5. Get some alone time with your baby while your partner is resting. Give her a bath, a bottle or just hold her to your heart. No quicker way to process it all than when she wraps her little hand around your finger.

6. Go for a walk - While some men may find it hard to tear themselves away from their newborn baby, others may need to remove themselves from the scene to take it all in. Take a walk in the hospital gardens, but try not to leave the premises. Bonus points if you come back with flowers for your partner.

7. Pray - For many men, a baby is the first time they acknowledge a God-like presence in their life. Take a moment to bow your head, and thank the universe for the bundle you have just received. Ask for the strength to be the best father you can be, and that your child deserves.

LIST #FIFTEEN:
NEW BABY CELEBRATION PROTOCOL

Having a new baby is a joyous time and although you feel like you should be allowed to just be lost in bonding with your offspring, there are some social protocols that must be followed:

1. Once your baby is out, don't just leave your partner on the delivery table with her legs hanging open. Stay close to her and watch her enjoy her first bonding moment with your child.

2. Mothers and mothers-in-law will be banging the door to the delivery room. Have a quick minute of privacy with your newborn child before you surrender her to the hoards.

3. Expect visitors as soon as the baby is born, whether you want them or not. Be prepared with a couple of bottles of champagne and celebratory sweets without your partner having to remind you to do so.

4. Your partner will want to look just like her old self as soon as the baby is born – tell her she does.

5. The day you bring your baby home, it is imperative to have something special in the house for your partner (See **LIST #TWENTY-EIGHT**).

6. Before your baby turns six weeks old, it is customary to send out a birth announcement. These can range from fancy and $10/piece, to easy and web-based (an email and a photo). They usually include the baby's name, date of birth, weight, length (optional), and something like "Mum not showing any signs of post-natal depression yet" or perhaps something less honest like "Mum and baby both happy and doing well".

7. If your culture has a baby welcoming ceremony, it usually happens within the first three months and will entail arranging invites, locations and caterers. Get on it, because chances are your partner will still be a bit overwhelmed initially. Get your mother to help if you must.

8. Your partner will want to do a family photo shoot at an overpriced studio that will charge you $200/print. Unless you know a professional photographer you owes you a favor, this is inevitable. However, try to

postpone it for the first six months because as much as you think your baby is adorable in the first week, they get much cuter as the months go on.

9. Within the first six months, it is good form to send out thank you cards or emails to all those wonderful people who brought or sent gifts.

10. If you live in Beverly Hills or the like, personalized baby stationery is obligatory. You can find free templates online, or go to your local stationer for more creative options.

NEW BABY AND YOU

LIST #SIXTEEN:
16 EMOTIONS YOU WILL EXPERIENCE AS A NEW DAD AND HOW NOT TO LET THEM OVERWHELM YOU

Paternal hormones are not a myth. As a new father, you will experience a range of emotions that may feel foreign to you. This coupled with the fact that everyone expects you to be in control while the rest of the household is falling apart can be quite trying. This list will help you understand what to expect.

1. Fear - The scariest thing that can happen to a man is fatherhood. The moment you feel the weightless baby in your hands, you feel the weight of the responsibility on your shoulders. Fear creeps through every bone in your body: What if I drop her? What if she gets hurt? How will I support a family? Am I cut out for this? The key is to focus on one day, or one moment at a time even. The fact that you are worried is a good sign.

2. Unbridled Pride - Having a child will feel like your proudest achievement and that's all good until you become that guy that's showing pictures of your son's first spit-up to the boys at the bar. Rein it in because it can get annoying, even to those closest to you.

3. Territorial - Childbirth brings out our raw, animal instincts. Involuntarily, you will become very protective of your partner, your child and your space. But get a grip: lots of people have had babies and know how to hold a newborn correctly – you don't have to hover.

4. Change of Focus - As a new dad, you will suddenly feel like nothing else in the world matters but being with your child. Former Type-A personalities or workaholics will be transformed into apron-clad, muffin-baking, Mrs. Doubtfires who drag their feet to the office. It's normal and understandable to not want to miss a moment of your new child's life. But the reality is that your partner has to stay home and someone has to pay the bills. So stop whining and get to work.

5. Paranoia - Perhaps because mothers claim to be blessed with "mother's intuition", fathers experience more palpable paranoia about their child's well being. What if something is wrong with him? What if he chokes on something and dies? What if he never knows his father because he is so wrapped up with mum? The reality is many things can go wrong but constantly worrying about them is only going to cripple your ability to respond. Babies are surprisingly resilient, and

you as a father become remarkably aware of how to protect your child with time and experience.

6. Poor - Having a child is an expensive proposition, even for the wealthier amongst us. Clothes, toys and baby gear are not cheap, not to mention hospital, obstetrician and other medical bills. Then there's kindergarten, school, college, and potentially graduate school. Not to mention insurances and retirement planning. It is overwhelming. The key is to start early. Many countries will offer tax benefits for educational savings. Seek some financial counseling on your options to put away money now for your kids to use in the future.

7. Unprepared - If you are a control freak, you better get used to ambiguity. Kids will throw you for a loop every time you think you know what's going on and be a step ahead of you all the time. The good news is that if you surrender to the lack of control, you are actually better prepared for change. Pay attention, listen for non-verbal cues, and remember that you may be unprepared, but you are not unaware.

8. Sober - Remember happy hour? Remember decadent boys' nights when you found yourself on someone else's floor? Someone else's bed? Yeah, all gone with a new baby (unless you are a crap father and not putting in your time). Now drunken nights out are few and far between and being hung over when you have to be up with the baby in the morning is less appealing than a stint on *The Fear Factor*. Sobriety can be unsettling but being up and clear-headed at seven am with your kid can be rewarding too.

9. Competitive - Whether you are the competitive sort or not, you will constantly be looking around to see how you stack up as a father. You will be competitive with your partner for the baby's attention and with other fathers to be the most involved one, with the most outstanding child. If you are aware of this feeling, you can rein it in and will have it under control by the time the baby is 6 months old.

10. Frustration - Sometimes not knowing what to do is a hard place for a man to be. There will be times when the baby won't settle or your partner won't settle and you are supposed to bear it all with a smile and a gift. Throw in a few months of sleep-deprivation and it's a recipe for disaster, or divorce. It's ok. Take a breath and call in reinforcements. Talk to a sibling, parent, or friend or go out to clear

your head. You deserve that, even though everyone forgets to tell you so.

11. Resentful - The politically correct thing for new parents to say is that parenthood is the best thing that has ever happened to them. But everyone who has had a child knows that it is hard work and a complete hijacking of your life, as you knew it. It's natural to resent that change sometimes. Know that this moment will pass and that you can get support from other people who have been through the same thing. 9 out of 10 times, a smile, gurgle or hug from your child will eradicate all doubt that this is worth it.

12. Left Out - The bond between a mother and a baby is special, how can it not be? It's natural for dad to feel left out particularly in the breast-feeding stages. But there is still a lot a dad can do to be involved: change diapers, take the baby for walks and offer to do night feeds with a bottle if that's an option. As the baby gets older, his/her dependency on mom becomes less and dad becomes an equal player as long as you are around and involved. So write off the first few months as evolution in play and dive right in to play your part.

13. Relief - A very real fear for dads is that something will happen to their partners during childbirth. While mum is totally consumed with the welfare of the baby, dads often feel lonely or selfish in their concern for their partners. It is perfectly normal to experience relief and a rush of emotion for your partner during this time. Express it to her, as it's important that she knows that she's more to you than a stork. (See **LIST #THIRTY**).

14. Ambitious - Dreams you may have never even had for yourself start inhibiting your daily thoughts as your child grows up. Just make sure that you don't become obsessive and suffocating. Exploring the world and having as varied experiences as possible is critical for the development of a young mind so curb your enthusiasm for a specific activity or interest till they've had a chance to look around for themselves a bit.

15. Rejected - When you think you are over the shock of having a new baby in your life (3 months-ish), give your partner at least double that to register the shock. This means that you are likely going to be enduring zero romance and even less sexual activity during that time. You have to understand what's just gone down (literally) with her body and give her time. Remember, it's not personal, it's just that Mother Nature has programmed her to focus solely on her child, the being that

needs the most care at this time. She'll get to you eventually, and if she doesn't after 6 months, ask for it. Chances are she will be ready for some adult loving too.

16. Vulnerable – Your typically invincible self is feeling a bit fragile, like you will be destroyed if anything took your partner and child away from you. This vulnerability can be unnerving, but it's all part of the process of fatherhood. Let yourself experience the ups and downs and you will be a better father, husband and human being for it. When it's time to "man up", you will.

LIST #SEVENTEEN:
11 SUREFIRE WAYS TO BUILD CONFIDENCE WITH YOUR CHILD

Dads sometimes don't believe they can be the primary caretakers. Do all of this by yourself and you're running the show!

1. Handle the morning wake-up - Change diaper, prepare milk, feed milk, find a way to entertain the kid while you get yourself some breakfast.

2. Put the baby down at naptime - Whatever your preferred method, get the baby to sleep as scheduled during the day.

3. Prepare 3 square meals and none of them come out of a jar, tin, or packet.

4. Feed the baby aforementioned meals.

5. Give the baby a bath, including brushing teeth, moisturizing, and cleaning up after.

6. Take the baby for a stroll in pram or baby carrier or to the park.

7. Run errands with the baby, like groceries or dropping off the dry cleaning or going to the doctor.

8. Take a work call, in which you have to explain at least once that you are home with your child and apologize for the noise and your scattered attention.

9. Change an explosive poop diaper, while the baby sticks his hands into the muck and you have to reach for wipes while trying to keep his fingers out of his mouth. Bonus points if this is done in front of an audience.

10. Comfort the baby through teething pains or a mild illness like fever or a stuffed up nose.

11. Give the baby a bath and a story before bed and still manage to have some energy to enjoy a glass of wine or bedtime activity with your partner.

LIST #EIGHTEEN:
12 PRODUCTIVE WAYS TO SPEND PATERNITY LEAVE

Having both of you in the house full-time fawning over the baby might create a case of "too many cooks". Here's how to not get into each other's hair but still make the most of quality family time:

1. Take over one activity with your child, be it feeding, bathing or reading, which will be exclusively your time with the baby.

2. Start planning for the future - Research educational savings funds.

3. Gather information from local parents about preschools and kindergartens and schedule interviews.

4. Rework your will to include your baby.

5. Build your child something like a swing or a play table and chair.

6. Take up gardening.

7. Read as many parenting books as you can - you will lose the time and the inclination once you get back to work.

8. Catch up with your friends - Having a social life and a full-time job is tough when you have a child so take the opportunity to invite your friends over or catch up over a coffee (with baby of course).

9. Learn to make a few quick but nutritious meals - This will come in handy mid-week when you are both exhausted at the end of the day.

10. Take your baby out for a walk every afternoon - It will be great bonding time for you both as well as give your partner some much needed rest and down time.

11. Stock up the freezer with some good home cooked food - It will come in handy on a night in the future when you are both hungry, the fridge is empty and you are too beat to cook.

12. Learn baby CPR.

LIST #NINETEEN:
10 WAYS TO KNOW IF "STAY-AT-HOME" DAD IS FOR YOU

If you answered "yes" to these questions, you are a great candidate to be a stay-at-home dad:

1. You don't mind listening to Sesame Street or singing "Twinkle Twinkle Little Star" all day.

2. You don't mind being the odd one out at the playground by being surrounded by mothers.

3. You are comfortable with your partner being the "bread winner" in the family.

4. You won't mind that, some days, your only outing may be to the grocery store.

5. You are ok with people being shocked and surprised that you have decided to be a stay-at-home dad.

6. Your idea of a successful day is getting the baby to nap for an hour extra so you could finish all the household chores you were behind on.

7. You won't feel left out by not having access to work mates.

8. It doesn't bother you that people may think that you are not actually "working".

9. You will not have any annual leave, lunch break or sick days off.

10. You are aware that it is one of the hardest jobs in the world and that you won't get paid a cent for it nor will you get any promotion. You may get a card on Father's Day.

LIST #TWENTY:
10 NEEDLESS WORRIES THAT PLAGUE NEW DADS

It's perfectly normal to have these thoughts, but realize that they are baseless as long as you are an attentive and caring father (and you must be, because you bought this book):

1. You will not like the baby.

2. The baby will not like you.

3. You will drop the baby.

4. You will not be able to provide for your new family (ok, this could happen without proper planning but the major costs associated with having a child don't kick in for the first few years which gives you time to plan).

5. You will forget the baby somewhere.

6. You will sleep through a feed and the baby will die.

7. You will break the baby's neck.

8. The baby will randomly stop breathing.

9. The baby will choke on your partner's breast.

10. Your partner will be moody and asexual forever (possible but unlikely).

LIST #TWENTY-ONE:
10 MISTAKES NEW FATHERS MAKE AND HOW TO AVOID THEM

It's inevitable - you will want to be perfect, and you won't be. Here's how new dads crack under pressure:

1. Sweating the small stuff - You can spend hours following instructions on how to wrap a baby or debating whether to burp him on his back or on his front. If you're getting wrapped up in the small stuff, you will be less effective, more frustrated and will miss out on the whole experience. Take a step back, relax, and focus on the end: to have a happy, healthy baby, not a regimented robot.

2. Trying to be perfect - People will constantly be judging you as a new father and bombarding you with unwanted advice making you feel like you have to perfect at all times. You don't, and in fact, you won't be, and the good news is, the more mistakes you make, the more you will learn.

3. Thinking your life won't change - Many men think that having a child is like buying a new TV; you love it when you're with it and you can turn it off when you are done. You can't. This being will take over your life and change all aspects of it. Eating, sleeping, travelling, socializing and living in general will be different (read: harder), so the sooner you accept that fact, the better.

4. Being too "by-the-book": Men being the natural problem solvers believe that when there is a problem, there is a solution. Books don't have all the answers and sometimes "old-wives' tales" or sheer gut instinct might save the day. Have an open mind.

5. Being too hands-off: Some fathers get intimidated by the thought of nurturing a newborn and let the mother face all the action. Being around and getting involved allows you some really critical bonding time, important for your development and that of the baby.

6. Being too hands-on: Don't knock mother's intuition. There is a bond between your child and your partner as they shared a body for 9 months that gives her a sense for what the baby needs. If you don't pick your battles, and act like you know everything about how to raise a child (even though you might, after this book), you set yourself up

as resistance instead of an ally. Sometimes you need to concede that mother knows best.

7. Expecting your single friends to "get it" - Your single friends will NOT understand why it's not easy for you to just leave the child with the babysitter, or why you can't stay out late when you're out, or why you talk about your baby all the time. These relationships will change; the good ones will evolve, and the bad ones will dissolve.

8. Standing behind the camera, not in front of it - Too many dads are so focused on capturing the moment that they forget to live it. Put the camera down, and go hug your child.

9. Ignoring your gut - Men will often doubt themselves as caregivers because our society doesn't give them much encouragement. Believe that you are a sensible, capable man, who wants nothing more than the best for your child, and follow your instincts. With time and confidence, the appropriate responses will come to you naturally.

10. Not asking for help - Many news dads feel like asking for help reveals their insecurity or incompetence as fathers. Quite the contrary, asking how to do something shows that you have the confidence to want to improve your knowledge and handling of the baby. Plus, your partner will be comforted that you can put your ego aside for the well being of your child. (News flash: she probably wants help too).

LIST #TWENTY-TWO:
THERAPIST OR THERA*PISSED*? - 10 QUESTIONS TO FIGURE OUT IF YOU ARE DOING TOO MUCH OR TOO LITTLE

1. Are you feeling like you are putting in your absolute best effort but can't get anything under control and the frustration is making you resent the child and your circumstances?

2. When somebody asks you how old your baby is, is your response "Umm... a few months"?

3. Does your partner constantly beg you to go out with your friends or take a night off?

4. Do you call your mum to come over every time you are left alone with the baby?

5. Are you so tired that you find yourself asleep at work and at the wheel?

6. Is your partner crying non-stop and you didn't notice?

7. Are you trying to breastfeed your baby with a strap-on boob (à la "Meet the Fockers")?

8. Does your neighbor know more about your child's routine than you do?

9. Does your partner feel like you are constantly competing for the baby's affection with her?

10. Does your child throw a screaming fit every time he is handed over to you?

If you answered "yes" to questions 1, 3, 5, 7, 9, you are probably getting in over your head and it's affecting your decision making and relationships. Take a step back and get some perspective.

If you answered "yes" to questions 2,4,6,8, 10 you need to step up your game and pay more attention to your partner and child or you will miss out on these formative years of parent-child bonding.

LIST #TWENTY-THREE:
8 WAYS TO CONTRIBUTE WITHOUT MISSING YOUR SUNDAY GOLF GAME

You can have it all! Here's how:

1. Schedule an afternoon tee time and take over the baby in the morning so she can sleep in.

2. Bring her breakfast in bed.

3. Plan dinner so that she doesn't have to spend the whole afternoon cooking yours.

4. Give her a night off to do whatever she wants to do. If she feels like she is having a bit of a life she won't resent you for wanting the same either.

5. Hire a babysitter, and send your partner to the spa if your golf club has one.

6. Encourage her to pursue her favorite activity once a week. If she's into photography, buy her admission to a photography course.

7. Pick up flowers or truffles on your way home.

8. Diamonds are atonement for any sin, as far as women are concerned.

MOTHERHOOD AND HER

LIST #TWENTY-FOUR:
10 THINGS NEVER TO SAY TO A NEW MOTHER

With her hormones going crazy and the general mayhem of a new baby household, your partner may be more sensitive than usual. Here are some statements that are sure to have you banished to the couch forever:

1. There is nothing you can do for the baby that I can't.

2. Are you sure breast milk is good for him? My mother gave me formula a lot and I turned out fine!

3. Do you think he looks like my father or my mother?

4. How come your stomach is so big even though the baby is out?

5. Microwave dinner *again* tonight?

6. Baby, I would love you even if your ass didn't look like cottage cheese.

7. How come you didn't have time to go to the grocery store? It's not like you are *working* at the moment.

8. Are you sure you want to have that drink? You don't want that to be the reason she doesn't go to Harvard.

9. You know, you are not the only one who is tired.

10. What do you mean your breasts aren't going to stay this big once you finish breastfeeding?

LIST #TWENTY-FIVE:
13 CONTROVERSIAL DECISIONS YOU SHOULD HAVE A SAY IN

Parenthood is a partnership. Here are some critical decisions that you should have an opinion on:

1. Pacifiers - The pacifier debate centers around how much you want to create a dependency on comfort aids, your threshold for unsettled babies and the potential of gum issues.

2. Routines - Some parents swear by routines and others let their babies automatically fall into them. You and your partner should decide what would work best with your life and parenting style.

3. Sleep Training - Similarly, sleep training is one of those hot topics that all parents have a strong opinion on. The idea of leaving your baby to cry himself to sleep can offend some, and be a boon to others. You and your partner need to decide if you're going to do it, when you're going to do it and for how long. Often, it's the father's strength that helps the mother stick through it.

4. Co-sleeping - There is mixed opinion around whether it is safe to share your bed with your baby and if it creates sleeping problems in the future. Unfortunately there is no right or wrong decision on this one, but it is known that a mother has never rolled over her newborn in a bed while some fathers have.

5. Bumpers - Bumpers in cribs are meant to be a risk for SIDS (Sudden Infant Death Syndrome). Your sense of spatial relationships will help assess the real threat for your child.

6. Costs - Both parents can be at fault for overspending on a new baby, and it's hardly a fair criticism as new parents are such a sucker market for retailers. That being said, you can be the voice of reason when things get out of hand. You really don't need a $2000 crib, unless it turns into a Porsche after 18 years.

7. Walkers - Walkers have been so controversial that they are actually banned in Canada. They have been criticized for causing accidents in children and for impeding the development of spatial and motor skills in babies. However, walkers have changed and been modified to eradicate factors that were issues in the past. Regardless, you and

your partner should both decide whether or not you want your child to use one.

8. Activities - You are a cellist, she is a gymnast. Or more likely, you are a sports freak, and she is an artist. It's important to have both parents' input so that the child gets a well-rounded education and is not forced into one activity or another too soon. Yes, we all secretly want our children to fulfill our dreams but we have to let them have their own dreams first.

9. Circumcision - Unless your religion or culture has a stand on circumcision, you will venture into the research and find that the official medical stand on the procedure waivers every 10 years. You and your partner should get the scientific low-down but there are two considerations that only a man can understand: Firstly, boys want to look the same as other boys in the locker room and secondly, boys want to look like their dads. If these two are in conflict, chances are you have a better shot at the right decision than your partner.

10. Immunization - Some people are not believers in immunization but choosing to vaccinate your child is definitely a joint decision to make. Be sure to consult your doctor if you decide not to immunize your child so you are fully aware of the risks associated.

11. Schools - From day cares to kindergarten and finally day school, the choices are daunting and the competition is stiff. You and your partner need to both be fully engaged.

12. Wills and contingency planning - What will happen to your baby if you and your partner die? It's a morbid but essential conversation to have.

13. Names – Naming your child is a decision that should be made jointly. Do you name him after your grandmother or do you branch out and introduce new names into the family? Refer to LIST #NINE for further guidance.

LIST #TWENTY-SIX:
7 IMPORTANT DECISIONS THAT ARE HERS TO MAKE

Yes it's your child, but it's not your body. There are some decisions that you just need to take a backseat on:

1. The birthing process: As much as you may like to stand on a soapbox and preach the virtues of vaginal deliveries, DON'T if your partner or circumstances have decided it will be a cesarean. Same goes for home births, water births, or any other seemingly unorthodox method of delivery she wants to pursue.

2. Epidurals and drugs in general: If you're feeling particularly self-righteous about this one, consider the fact that it's not you that's going to pass a watermelon through your nether bits. Modern medicine has advanced a great deal since the medieval days and options offered to women in legit institutions are safe for mum and the baby. If she wants to be knocked unconscious at the onset of labor and revived when the baby is safely in her arms, so be it.

3. Who witnesses the birth: Again, it's only fair that she picks whether or not she wants an audience. If it's just you and the doc, or her entire book club, it's her decision.

4. Obstetrician: While it is great for you to be familiar with your partner's obstetrician, it is not essential for you to love him. If your partner likes him, go with the flow, and please resist the urge for the "I told you so" if something goes wrong. Refer to **LIST #THREE** for signs that she needs to change her ob/gyn.

5. Breast-feeding or not: It is your partner's prerogative to decide whether or not she will breastfeed her child. Despite the proven benefits of breast-feeding, some women will choose not to breastfeed either for lifestyle reasons, or because they are simply unable to. Trust that she will do the best she can for your child.

6. Breast-feeding in public: Many men are uncomfortable with the notion of their partner's breasts on display but you have to understand the inconvenience and social isolation linked with having to leave the table/room/restaurant every time you have to nurse. The women that have the best time breastfeeding are the ones whose partners are

completely comfortable with and proud of the fact that they are. (Note: breastfeeding in public is not acceptable in some cultures).

7. Your first visitors: When you bring the baby home from hospital, your partner's focus will be on the baby, but you need to still focus on your partner as she will need a lot of care, both mentally and emotionally. Therefore, particularly if this is your first child, it is normal for her to want her family to be the ones present to get her through this overwhelming time in her life. *Cautionary Note*: Do not think that having both your mothers there at the same time is a compromise - you will be suicidal or divorced or both by the end of it.

LIST #TWENTY-SEVEN:
12 FREAKY THINGS PREGNANCY AND CHILDBIRTH CAN DO TO HER BODY

No, she's not Frankenstein. And try to conceal your shock, it's not like she's doing it on purpose!

1. Schizoid nipples - Pregnancy does weird things with pigmentation in your body. Pink nipples become purple and hazelnut ones become chocolate. Your partner's nipples may also grow to cover larger areas of her breasts than you could imagine possible. Don't worry, it's normal.

2. Line down the stomach - The *Treasure Trail* that has no scientific explanation is a line that appears from your partner's navel (or higher) down to the pubic bone. It's like nature trying to point out all the organs of her body that are working overtime. It's normal and it usually goes away after the baby is born.

3. Hemorrhoids - Every woman's fear, every man's contraceptive. Also called *piles* because too much pressure in that region causes skin tissue to herniate and stick out like grapes, or *piles* of grapes. They hurt, they itch, they burn, and they can show up at any point in the pregnancy (including during the actual delivery). All in all, if your partner has hemorrhoids you can forget about anal sex if you were ever into that sort of thing, and generally expect her to be in a fair bit of pain till they make their way back up where they belong. Sometimes surgery is the only corrective option.

4. Random, sprouty hair - If your partner was previously smooth and hair-free don't freak out if she suddenly starts sprouting single or tufts of hair on her chin, back, nipples or other parts of her body. It's the hormones and if they don't settle after the pregnancy there are always permanent hair removal treatments.

5. Incontinence - Yep, it's the same one that old people have and the reason they make adult diapers. All that pressure and pushing weakens the pelvic floor muscles so that your partner may leak while coughing, laughing, dancing, or just hanging out. And by the way, this is a pre and post-delivery effect.

6. Expanded vagina - One reason elective caesareans are becoming more and more popular.

7. Leaky breasts - While your partner is nursing, she will get used to her boobs leaking at random moments: when the baby cries, when the weather gets a bit warm, when she is stimulated even in the slightest. This magical phenomenon does not stop once she stops nursing - she could be a leaky faucet for up to a few months after.

8. Teenage acne - If you married your high-school sweetheart you are in luck - she may be back! High hormone levels can lead to outbreaks in some women that will make her face look like the dark side of the moon. Once again the line is, "You look beautiful darling!" no matter what.

9. Spider veins - All that pressure on the legs causes bluish-red varicose veins to show up in objection. They usually become worse towards to the end of the pregnancy.

10. Cankles - This is when her feet get so swollen that the delicate arch that leads from the calves to the ankles disappears and you are left with a giant elephant foot. This usually happens later in the pregnancy and most women go back to their original size after delivery.

11. Stretch marks - The good news is that these are genetic, the bad news is that it's probably too late to check your mother-in-law out. Stretch marks occur when the skin expands but loses some of its elasticity on the way back down. They can be purple, white or greyish and will be runs in your partner's skin and self-esteem. Expensive creams and lotions won't work (See **LIST #FIVE**).

12. Weird food cravings: It's cute when it's ice creams and pickles (less so when it's those things together), but pregnancy cravings in extreme cases can go beyond weird to bizarre. Some women have reported chalk cravings (for calcium) and brick cravings (for iron). If you see your partner chatting up a schoolteacher or construction worker, beware!

LIST #TWENTY-EIGHT:
10 UNIQUE IDEAS FOR A PUSH PRESENT THAT WILL KEEP HER PUSHING

For those of you not in the know, you picked this book up just in time. A "Push Present" is what you buy your partner as a "thank-you" for going through the process of delivering your child. Applies even if she didn't technically "push".

1. A ten-pack of massages at her favorite spa. While you may consider this a luxury, it will be a godsend for your partner whose every muscle will be aching from carrying and nursing your baby. Plus, her hips and legs may be sore for up to six weeks after delivery.

2. A gift voucher for her favorite shoe or handbag store. Her body won't be the same for a while after delivery so she may not appreciate new clothes. However the right shoes and bags can make any overweight frump look sexy.

3. Upgrade your cable TV subscription to include movie channels and anything that features Oprah and George Clooney. You will be spending many more nights in front of the tube.

4. A new TV (see above). This could also double up as a present for you!

5. A washing machine or a dishwasher if you don't already have one. You will be amazed at how many clothes and dishes you will go through.

6. Hire a cleaner or a cook or both. The work piles up when you have a baby and you will find that your partner will be so much happier (and possibly friskier), if some of the load is taken off her.

7. If you are thinking about going big and buying her a new car, consider getting her something sexy like a Mini Cooper or a BMW. An SUV is practical but it's a glaring reminder that she is more soccer mom than MILF, and for heaven's sake, no minivans.

8. Sunday sleep-ins for the first six months (come on, you still get Saturdays and you don't have cankles. See **LIST #TWENTY-SEVEN**).

9. A one-way ticket to visit her mum (with the baby) if she lives in another country, state or city. The one-way bit is important because it shows that you are truly putting her interests above yours.

10. Diamonds are of course, a girl's best friend, or anything that comes in a blue Tiffany box.

LIST #TWENTY-NINE:
9 WORST PUSH PRESENT IDEAS

Remember that a push present is supposed to make her feel good, not bad! Here's how you can really blow it:

1. Lingerie: Let's face it, she's fat and hairy and doesn't look anything like a Victoria's Secret model.

2. An iron (In fact, that's a crap present for any occasion).

3. Jenny Craig weight loss program subscription.

4. The "sports" upgrade on cable TV.

5. A one-way ticket for your mother to visit.

6. A thong bikini.

7. A golf trip for you to "get out of her hair".

8. A surprise "Welcome Home" party where you proceed to get hammered with your buddies and she has to clean up while you are passed out, drooling on the couch.

9. A mistress.

LIST #THIRTY:
10 NEGATIVE EMOTIONS SHE WILL EXPERIENCE POST-DELIVERY AND HOW TO HANDLE THEM

Most men believe that the end of the pregnancy is the end of the Frankenstein era, but many people (including new mothers) underestimate the emotional roller coaster that is the post-baby phase. Here's how to ride it and survive:

1. Insecure- The pressure on new mums is intense. Everyone expects them to feel motherly and develop that famous intuition within seconds of popping the baby out. She will constantly be wondering if she is a good mother and if people are watching her thinking she is incompetent. It is critical that you make her feel confident in her handling of the baby. Praise her often and respect her decisions with regards to the baby's care.

2. Ugly - When you have overhang like a sumo wrestler and no baby inside to blame it on, your ego takes a beating. Plus the hormones are still wreaking havoc on your skin, your hair is falling, your nails are chipped and your boobs are the Niagara Falls. As the husband, it is your job to remind her how much you love her, and to gently nudge her out of the slump (ever so gently... a gym membership can backfire so tread very cautiously).

3. Worthless - When you are pregnant for 9 months, you are put on a pedestal by your partner, your families, and even by random strangers on the bus. Once the baby's done, boom, you hit reality in all its mundane glory and realize that you are not so special anymore. Plus you are fat and balding (see above) and sleep deprived. She will need to be reminded her of why you are with her and how she would be so special to you, even if she hadn't borne you the child you are now obsessed with.

4. Used - Many women feel like they are treated as baby-popping machines, and that no one cares about them once the baby has been (signed, sealed, and) delivered. That's one of the main reasons for the onset of post-baby blues. They feel like they have given up their lives and bodies for this creature and no one appreciates them for it. Show her otherwise, it can only reap rewards in your marriage.

5. Trapped - All of a sudden, the reality of the commitment that is a child sets in. She's acutely aware that never again will she able to leave the

office and meet a friend for a drink, make a play for a VP position at work, or even just get her nails done, without major strings attached. Overnight, guilt and babysitters and breast pumps have overrun her footloose existence. It is very critical that you help her through this by supporting her return to work when she is ready, and encouraging her to take up activities she used to enjoy.

6. Pressurized - Everyone thinks they know how to do it better and even other mothers pile on the pressure when they sit together and compare their babies' height, weight and overall development. Your partner will feel conflicted between all the pieces of advice flying in from everywhere, and frustrated because she doesn't always magically know the right answer. This gets worse if you have a baby who is colicky or fussy, when she will feel particularly incompetent as a mother. Take the edge off by giving her some time off every day, and by reminding her to trust her instincts.

7. Unsuccessful - If your partner is used to calling the shots in the boardroom, she is not going to adjust well to not being in control at home. While many women struggle with going back to work after a baby is born, many also suffer from depression because of the seemingly mutually exclusive child and career relationship. It may add to the frustration that she wants to get back to work but finds herself sleep-deprived and exhausted most of the time. As a partner, you need to support her decision to go back to work, and to be cognizant of not always putting your career before hers when someone has to stay home to look after the baby.

8. Conflicted - She really wants to get on with her life, because being a "homemaker" is not always enough for women in this day and age, but she is having a hard time breaking away and can't imagine anyone else caring for her baby. She cries all day at work, and then worries about it at home, and generally feels like no one is getting the best of her. This is a tough one that very few women can honestly say they have figured out. But all the ones who have have partners who understand and support their needs.

9. Over-The-Hill: "Mother" is a whole new level of unavailable. Most men will run and hide when you say you are a mom because they imagine you cooking Chef Boyardee and smelling like laundry detergent. They are not far off. But her sudden drop in "fuckability" will make your partner feel old and frumpy, especially compared with the perky 23-

year olds whose breasts don't sag to their knees that now hang around the joints you used to frequent. Try to make her feel young and special by bringing back the magic and spontaneity of your courtship days.

10. Just plain exhausted: By the time your baby is six months old, she would not have slept a full night for about 240 days (the last two months of pregnancy are fraught with cramps and frequent trips to the bathroom). That can wreak havoc on anyone's mood and concentration. For the welfare of your partner and for your own sanity (because we all know how closely they are linked), you have to pitch in with the work, both physical and mental. Nobody told her that the hardest part comes after the baby is born, and she is realizing that the hard way. Be compassionate, be helpful, and most of all, BE THERE.

LIST #THIRTY-ONE:
7 WAYS TO COMBAT POSTPARTUM DEPRESSION
(AKA POST-BABY BLUES)

Postpartum depression is a serious pathology affecting more women than is publicly acknowledged. Keep your family from becoming a statistic and address the problem proactively:

1. Admit the problem - Accept that your partner may be suffering from a condition that cannot and should not be ignored. Postnatal depression is a state that needs treatment. You owe it to your beautiful new baby, you partner, your family and yourself to treat it seriously.

2. Talk about it - One of the symptoms of depression is the inability to get things done. This interferes with the most important part of the treatment, which is seeing someone about it. It is crucial to sit and talk about it with someone who knows the condition and can treat it. And like anything, the sooner, the better.

3. Get counseling – A partner with postpartum depression and a new baby is a lot to handle. Make sure you can handle it by getting some professional help.

4. Get some help with your baby - PPD is often linked to exhaustion. If you can't take some time off work to help look after your baby, then get someone who can. It is important for your partner to not have the entire burden of looking after the baby as she needs to take care of herself a little more than usual.

5. Join a self-help group: Problems are much better dealt with if shared. And it will also highlight that there are many other people going through exactly the same situation. Contact your local community center or doctor to figure out where to find the nearest group.

6. Consider antidepressant medicines: Antidepressant drugs can be a huge help as they destabilize the chemical balance within the brain and this elevates your mood. DO NOT TAKE ANYTHING WITHOUT CHECKING WITH YOUR DOCTOR and be sure to ask about side effects and whether she should stop breastfeeding.

7. Consider stress management: Post-natal depression is also a disease of stress, so stress management tools can be used to control it. Try

and get her to relax using tools like meditation and breathing techniques.

LIST #THIRTY-TWO:
9 REASONS "IT'S NOT YOU, IT'S ME" ISN'T JUST A LINE

Many men feel rejected when their partners fail to show any interest in resuming a healthy sex life months after the baby is born. Here's why not to take it personally:

1. She has hemorrhoids.

2. She is still sore from the delivery (this is possible for up to 6 months after).

3. She had an episiotomy (stitches on her vagina).

4. She is still bleeding and it's freaking her out.

5. She is not comfortable with her post-baby body (it takes nine months to put on the weight and for most women, at least that long to shed it).

6. The drop in hormones is making her feel depressed.

7. Her breasts are still leaking, and she is worried about putting you off.

8. Hormonal changes and breastfeeding have dried out her vagina (not forever, but it's not as lubricated as it used to be).

9. She is plain exhausted (See **LIST #THIRTY-THREE**).

LIST #THIRTY-THREE:
10 WAYS TO GET LAID POST-BABY

Below are some quick tips to get your sex life back on track. Note: you may have to do some combination or all of these before you see results:

1. Get a cleaning person in for the day.

2. Do the laundry and the groceries.

3. Buy her a voucher to get her hair and nails done, while you babysit.

4. Going out might be more of a stress, so plan a night at home where you cook her dinner, let her relax while you do the dishes and then give her a massage.

5. Take the night shift of feeding the baby.

6. Take the early morning shift too (hey, nobody said this was going to be easy).

7. Remind her of how sexy she is to you - chances are she may have forgotten.

8. Have an honest conversation about how you would like to refocus on the relationship between the two of you as soon as she is ready. That will get her thinking about it (your sensitivity and patience might guilt her into surrendering).

9. Bribe your partner with an expensive gift so she will feel bad denying you something for free (it's low, but effective!).

10. Beg.

OTHER RELATIONSHIPS

LIST #THIRTY-FOUR:
7 PEOPLE NOT TO TAKE BABY ADVICE FROM

When it comes to babies, everyone's an expert! Except for these people:

1. Anyone whose child is a spoiled brat.

2. People who laugh as their children beat up other kids at the park.

3. Men who think Mothers' Groups are a place to meet chicks.

4. Pregnant women who smoke or do drugs.

5. Your bud that has had longer relationships with cartons of milk than with any woman.

6. Your 10-year old niece (even though she is female and *sounds* like she knows what she is talking about).

7. Anyone who stares at your partner's breasts while she is nursing.

LIST #THIRTY-FIVE:
8 WAYS TO STILL HAVE A SOCIAL LIFE WHEN YOU HAVE A NEW CHILD

If you thought life wouldn't change after you had a baby, you're in for a shock. Follow the tips below to resuscitate the biggest casualty of childbirth, your social life:

1. Lower your standards - If you were a catering and seven-course meal kind of couple, forget about it for now. Invite people over and ask them to bring something or order in, and use paper plates so you are not scrubbing and wiping after they leave. Same goes for eating out - you will be stressed out if your child misbehaves in a five-star restaurant so keep it casual when you are dining out with baby.

2. Do weekend brunch - Make the most of your days if you know that the baby is fussier in the evening (as most babies are). Weekend brunches are usually family affairs so restaurants tend to have baby-friendly meals and crowds.

3. Meet people with kids - They know what you are going through so you are not completely embarrassed when the baby spits up his last meal all over the table.

4. Take turns giving each other a break - You both need time off from parenting and if you can't get it together, at least get it on your own. She can babysit while you take a night out with the boys and vice versa. This is the time to catch up with your non-parent friends. Note that hangovers are still not a good idea.

5. Make the most of grandparents - Take the opportunity to let mum and dad bond with their grandchild and take your partner out to meet some friends or for a quiet dinner.

6. Meet at people's homes - Homes are much easier because there is always a clean bathroom at hand.

7. Have one babysitter and 2 back-ups in case you get bailed on on your one and only night out.

8. Buy a pram with a bassinet and head out to dinner while the baby is sleeping (only doable till the baby is about 6 months old).

LIST #THIRTY-SIX:
10 WAYS TO MAKE NICE WITH YOUR MOTHER-IN-LAW WHEN YOU WANT TO JUST STUFF HER INTO THE MICROWAVE STERILIZER

It's the one time that you will be forced to interact extensively with your mother-in-law, and for the sake of your partner, you have to find a way to make it workable. Here's what you can do:

1. Designate specific chores for her so she feels like she is being involved, but is kept out of your hair.

2. If she is overly critical, thank her for her input but explain to her the concept of "constructive criticism".

3. Give her alone time with the baby and ensure that she gives you the same.

4. Send her out with your partner once a week so that you are dad in charge on some regular basis (2 birds!).

5. Leave her to babysit while you take your partner out.

6. Pick your battles. You will drive yourself insane if you react to every petty comment.

7. Understand her perspective: in her day, men were not involved in raising children, so your having an opinion (and a strong one at that) may confuse her.

8. Win her over with a gift: She is after all the mother of the child who is the mother of your child. She will like that you remember that.

9. Try to learn all you can: Unless your partner thinks she was the worst mother in the world, try to sponge up her advice about raising children. The more information you have, the better your decisions as a father will be. At minimum it will give you some insight into your partner's parenting style.

10. Discuss with your partner how she would like you to address any issue you have with her mother: she may be too exhausted to care, or may choose to mediate to prevent you both from sulking for a week.

LIST #THIRTY-SEVEN:
10 WAYS TO REIN IN YOUR MOTHER BEFORE YOUR PARTNER THROWS THE BREAST PUMP AT HER

Tensions may be high between your partner and your mother, and they're both looking at you to mediate. Here's how you can do it without pissing off either of your girls:

1. Talk to your mother before the baby is born about things your partner feels strongly about and that are considered non-negotiable.

2. Praise your partner's parenting style in the presence of your mother, especially when you know she is about to criticize something.

3. Designate specific tasks for your mother so she feels like she is contributing (cooking, knitting, shopping).

4. Ask your partner how she wants to handle the conflict: with you as mediator, or directly in her own potentially lethal, hormonal way?

5. Leave grandma to babysit or take the baby for a walk so you two have some quiet and alone time.

6. Remind her that you and your partner are responsible adults that are confident about all the decisions you have made (even if you are not).

7. Make sure you, your partner and the baby have some alone time together.

8. Promote time staying with your parents as "time-off" for your partner, when she can get a massage, do her nails or go shopping, guilt-free.

9. Permit your partner to blatantly ignore your mother if the latter makes comments about the former's looks, career, cooking or next child.

10. Request your partner to cut mum some slack – she is probably overwhelmed with the emotion just like you both are (this is especially permissible for a first grandchild).

BABY CARE

LIST #THIRTY-EIGHT:
9 STEPS TO CHOOSING A PEDIATRICIAN

Choosing your child's pediatrician is a difficult decision, as you can never tell how good they are until you really need them. Here are a few tips to help your assessment:

1. Ask all your friends and family with kids whom they like - this is one area in which referrals make a huge difference.

2. Schedule interviews with three or four doctors, ideally in your neighborhood. Last thing you need is a long drive for an emergency consultation.

3. Assess their approach to medicine - are they pill pushers? Or are they inclined to let minor things sort themselves out?

4. How much time they are willing to spend with you during the consultation is an indication of how rushed your appointments will be.

5. Look at the state of the consulting rooms and the receptionist - if either of them is shabby or off-putting, keep looking.

6. Ask about after-hours and emergency care - when and how will they be available?

7. Learn their opinions on topics that are important to you such as circumcision, immunizations and home remedies.

8. Meet any other doctors they are affiliated with, to know whom you might get if he/she is unavailable.

9. If you baby is born already, watch how the doctor handles them: if the baby is comfortable with her, it's a good sign.

LIST #THIRTY-NINE:
12 THINGS YOU MUST KNOW ABOUT BREASTFEEDING

Having a partner who is supportive and informed is a great help to a nursing mother. Impress her by showing that you know that boobs are good for more than just fun:

1. The removal of the placenta is the trigger for the milk to start flowing in a woman's body. This may take 2-3 days, during which time it is perfectly natural for the baby to remain unfed. If your baby is premature, doctors may start him on formula to reduce the risk of weight gain.

2. The yellowy substance that flows before the milk does is called colostrum and is very heavy in fat, so smaller amounts of it fill the baby up faster than regular breast milk.

3. Babies and new mothers have to learn the art of breastfeeding, as it's not something that you just wake up knowing how to do. Learning stages can be frustrating and painful for a first time mother.

4. Breastfeeding works on demand and supply: the more the baby drinks, the more the breasts will supply. That's why doctors recommend pumping between feeds to increase milk production.

5. The amount of milk you produce is directly correlated with how much water your partner drinks - breast milk is basically a combination of water and food.

6. Babies can have very sensitive stomachs and even allergies to things like dairy, which make it very hard on a breastfeeding mother.

7. In the early days, breastfeeding takes time. If your baby is on a three-hour schedule it is calculated three hours from when you start, not when you finish. This means that your partner can start feeding at 2am and take up to an hour or more to feed, burp and resettle the baby and then she is on again at 5. And you wonder why she is not up for a quickie! The good news is that babies become more efficient feeders as they get older.

8. It is common for one breast to be a better producer than the other.

9. Breast milk can be stored in the refrigerator for up to 72 hours and in the deep freeze up to 6 months. Ice cube containers or plastic storage bags can be used to freeze milk. Once defrosted, this milk must be consumed immediately and only heated up once. Treat it like gold, your partner as good as bleeds to produce that milk.

10. Breastfeeding going wrong produces a condition called mastitis, which can be extremely painful for your partner. It is an inflammation of the breast tissue caused by blocked milk ducts. Mastitis can be cured by antibiotics and massages and continual feeding (painful!) to help open up the blockage.

11. Breast pumps come in all shapes, brands and prices. Hand-operated, electrical, single-handed, double-handed. Do your research to find out what works for you.

12. If your partner chooses not to breastfeed, be prepared to feel a bit left out of the crowd. There is a big push these days to encourage breast feeding in new mums so don't feel bad about the pressure if you know you have made the right decision for your partner and your baby.

LIST #FORTY:
10 EASY WAYS TO ALLEVIATE COMMON DISCOMFORT IN YOUR BABY

As a new parent, the slightest sign of discomfort can send you into a panic. Follow the signs below to alleviate common symptoms in newborn babies. And always, when in doubt, call your doctor.

1. Gas - It's amazing how often babies take into too much air while feeding and get all riled up about it. If this occurs, your baby will need to be burped. Refer to the bonus lists section for the most effective ways to burp your baby.

2. Colic - There are a lot of theories regarding colic and its treatment. But generally the most obvious symptom of colic is continuous crying, particularly in the evening hours. The treatment recommended is simply calming your baby down by removing excessive stimulation and using the techniques in **LIST #FORTY-ONE.**

3. Reflux - Acid reflux in babies is the same in babies as it is in adults - and can actually be treated by the same meds, in smaller doses, but with a doctor's consent. There are also simple things you can do to help the baby's digestion: raise the cot to an angle so that the food is encouraged to stay down by gravity, keep the baby upright for about half an hour after a feed, cut out foods that might be harder to digest if you are nursing, or supplement with a hydrolyzed formula.

4. Blocked Nose - Your baby's nasal passage is so small that almost anything can clog it up. Air conditioning tends to dry out the air so invest in a humidifier if that's the cause. Saline drops also act as a natural decongestant. They can be bought over the counter at any drug store and are very effective when used with an aspirator.

5. Ear Infection - You will know if your baby has an ear infection because she will keep touching her ears. Take her to a doctor for a prescription and refrain from activities such as swimming.

6. Nappy Rash - Some babies are more prone to it than others and it generally occurs when a baby stays in a dirty diaper for too long. A general rule of thumb is to change every feed or every four hours, if you don't receive any other indication that you need to change the

diaper. There are several good nappy rash creams on the market and petroleum jelly like Vaseline can help reduce chaffing if the baby is extra sensitive. You want to keep the area clean and dry all the time.

7. Hunger - Easy fix and feeding should be your first defense if the baby is crying seemingly without reason. Adults don't get hungry on a schedule, so why should babies? Just pop in a boob or a bottle and watch them revert back to angel-mode.

8. Hot/Cold - Babies don't know how to regulate their body temperature so it's not uncommon for them to be sweating when it's snowing outside. If they look like they are going red or breaking out into a rash, they might be too hot, or if their noses feel cold to touch, they need another blanket or layer of clothing.

9. Attention - Books will teach you to train your baby from a young age to self-soothe and to be independent. Well, if they were going to be independent, they may as well get up and get a job! Babies are social creatures and they need physical proximity to feel reassured in their relatively new surroundings. If your baby is crying uncontrollably and you have eliminated any ailments, pick her up and hold her close to you - that might be all she is asking for.

10. Constipation - If your baby is purely breastfed, she can go up to a week without pooping. In formula-fed babies it is more important to get them going regularly. A bit of apple or prune juice mixed with water in equal proportions, some rectal stimulation with a rectal thermometer or simply massaging the stomach may do the trick.

LIST #FORTY-ONE:
WHAT TO DO WHEN YOUR BABY (AND YOUR PARTNER)
WON'T STOP CRYING!

When it feels like it should be "all hands on deck" and the only ones available are yours, roll up your sleeves and take control:

1. Send visiting relatives home. If you have an older child, send him with them.

2. Stick a note on the front door saying that you are out.

3. Go into your baby's room, draw the blinds, and make the light in the room dim.

4. Put on some quiet, restful music (that's for you). Babies do like a background of 'family sounds' rather than silence.

5. Feed him on demand in the dim light, avoiding long periods of eye contact with him.

6. After the feed, wrap him firmly, ideally with his back rounded and limbs contained - this will remind him of the warmth of the womb and help him feel secure. He may want to have his arms free, but it is preferable to hold them in.

7. Place him in his cot, on his side, facing the wall. Pat him gently on the bottom at about 70 pats to the minute (mother's heart rate) and just bore him to sleep!

8. If you're using one, give him a pacifier.

9. When all fails, pop him into the car and go for a long drive. Nothing soothes babies faster than movement. This has the added benefit of giving your partner some privacy to collect herself.

10. Do not leave your baby to cry, but you can leave the room when he finally settles.

11. Repeat the above steps on your partner.

LIST #FORTY-TWO:
12 SUREFIRE WAYS TO GET YOUR BABY TO SLEEP THROUGH THE NIGHT

It's the goose with golden eggs, the newborn that sleeps through the night, and hopefully these tricks will help you get close to one:

1. Try to put your baby to sleep when he/she shows the first signs of tiredness such as yawning, a fixed stare, avoiding eye contact, rubbing eyes, or jerky leg movements. It is important to put your baby to sleep before she becomes overtired.

2. Movement: Your baby is used to being rocked for at least 16 hours a day inside your partner's womb, so being left lying still in a bassinette will be very strange for her! You can easily replicate womb movement by rocking or jiggling your baby, which is an excellent way to calm crying and help her nod off in the first few weeks. If your baby really needs movement to fall asleep, try a bouncinette, sling, front pack, or an electric swing. If you are using movement, you will find combining swaddling and movement is much more effective. We recommend that you only use movement in the first couple of months, and only when your baby really needs it to get to sleep. You want to start creating independent sleeping habits as soon as possible.

3. Feeding: If your baby is really tired and struggling to settle, feeding may be just what is needed to get her to nod off. Breast milk is particularly good for making babies drowsy, so it's quite common for tired newborns to drift off while feeding. However babies who are fed to sleep can sometimes wake quite soon after, either with wind or because the nice, warm milk is no longer there so use it wisely.

4. Roll your baby onto her side, and firmly and rhythmically pat her back. If she is struggling to fall asleep it may take quite a few minutes before you see an impact of your patting. This can be a good technique as your baby gets older and you want to rely less on rocking or feeding to get to sleep.

5. The best routine for a newborn baby is feed, play, and sleep. This way, your baby will not think that she needs to feed to fall asleep and when she wakes, you will know that she is hungry.

6. Swaddle your baby - Swaddling is one of the best techniques to get your baby to sleep through the night. A swaddle emulates the feeling in the womb as your baby is tightly wrapped. The wrap also prevents your baby from waking herself from their startle reflex.

7. Set predictable and consistent nap routines. Babies are creatures of habit and usually recognize and respond very well to regularity.

8. The best way you get your baby to sleep through the night is by teaching her to self-settle. Babies usually experience a sleep cycle of about 45 minutes after which they are fully awake. Teaching your baby to go back to sleep without you or a sleeping aid will ensure that she can put herself back to sleep between cycles.

9. Play some white noise. You can purchase cds of white noise, which emulate sounds from inside the womb. This may sound very strange and seem even more unlikely to work, but believe it or not, it actually does! Further, when you have already experienced months of constant interrupted sleep, you will try anything and often this is just the answer!

10. Back patting - If you want to put your baby into bed awake or they need help to resettle once in bed, back-patting can be very effective. Combine this technique with swaddling, white noise and possibly a pacifier.

11. Give your baby a pacifier. Pacifiers can be an absolute godsend and can make for a much happier baby and therefore parents! In the USA, it is now recommended that all babies use a pacifier as research has shown reduced risk of SIDS for dummy users. However, avoid introducing it until breastfeeding is well established, and always offer once baby has been calmed with swaddling, side/stomach patting and white noise (rather than putting it in while your baby is screaming!).

12. Forehead stroking - One of the best secrets for getting a baby to nod off is stroking their forehead. Swaddle first, put on some white noise and pop in the pacifier if using one. Then gently stroke your baby's forehead, from the bridge of the nose upwards. It works much better to go upwards, rather than downwards which is more commonly used. Stroking in a small circle can also work well for some babies.

LIST #FORTY-THREE:
20 REASONS TO CALL YOUR DOCTOR

Below is a list of signs that your baby needs to see a doctor. It is important to note that if your child is experiencing something that is not mentioned below and you are worried, seek medical advice anyway. Better to be safe than sorry.

1. Your child's respiratory rate is 60 or more per minute maintained over five minutes or more.

2. Your child's temperature is higher than 101F or below 96.8F.

3. Fits or convulsions.

4. Fewer than 2 wet nappies per day.

5. Increasing jaundice beyond one week of age.

6. Obvious blood in stool or urine beyond one week of age.

7. A pale complexion.

8. Listless behavior.

9. Refusal to feed.

10. A combination of vomiting and diarrhea.

11. Repeated projectile vomiting.

12. Any vomiting of bile.

13. Symmetrical red inflammation around the base of the stump of the umbilical cord.

14. Difficulty breathing, with in-drawing from the chest.

15. A high fever with no other symptoms.

16. Barking, 'seal-like' cough.

17. Blue fingernails and toenails (beyond the first day of birth).

18. Unusual excessive crying.

19. Your baby's limbs don't move symmetrically.

20. Your baby doesn't look right (your parental instincts will let you know).

LIST #FORTY-FOUR:
10 TOYS YOUR NEWBORN WILL LOVE (NOT NECESSARILY AVAILABLE AT A TOY STORE)

Parents spend thousands on toys for their children only to find that the real entertainers are under their very noses (and usually free)!

1. Keys

2. Remote control for the TV

3. Empty water bottle filled with colored dried pasta, rice, or anything colorful that makes a noise when the bottled is shaken (be careful that the contents cannot choke the baby in the event that the bottle breaks or the lid comes off).

4. Cell phone

5. Stickers

6. Your wallet

7. Pots and pans and a spoon (HEAVEN!)

8. Anything with buttons

9. YouTube!

10. Bubbles

TRAVEL

LIST #FORTY-FIVE:
10 TIPS FOR YOUR FIRST TRIP WITH BABY

Whether it's a transcontinental flight or a two-hour drive to grandma's, your first trip with the baby can be a frightening experience. Follow these steps to ensure it's not hell on Earth:

1. Make sure your baby is in a structured routine well before you travel. This makes it far easier to ensure your baby doesn't get overtired and you always know what you need to do for baby, wherever you are or whatever you are doing!

2. Ensure she is used to whatever she will be sleeping in while you are away.

3. Get your baby well rested before you travel. You may have a lot of rushing around to do before you go, but try not to drag her around the shops or miss her naps while you madly rushing to get ready.

4. Do not try new foods on a holiday. Always feed her things she has tried before and that you know agree with her.

5. Book flights at times that fit her routine as going through customs with a baby at feed-time is a sure recipe for disaster! This is particularly easy with domestic flights, when there are lots to choose from.

6. If your baby is no longer swaddled, make sure she is using a baby sleeping bag, so her sleeping environment will be the same every night.

7. If you are travelling internationally, make sure you check up on the availability of baby products.

8. Buy a stroller she can sleep comfortably in, so she can nap while you are on the go.

9. Try to avoid falling into bad habits while you are away. Whilst it may be very tempting to feed your baby to sleep or pick her up the instant she starts crying, you will pay the price when you return home.

10. Make sure you travel with your baby's favorite toy / blanket. Babies pick up on stressful situations, so having her favorite toy will be a savior when things just aren't going your way e.g. your plane has been delayed or you have missed your connecting flight. It is also something familiar for them to hold in a strange environment. If you have the space to spare, it is even better if you can have a couple extras up your sleeve, in case it mysteriously goes missing which is highly likely in transit.

LIST #FORTY-SIX:
8 CONSIDERATIONS FOR INTERNATIONAL TRAVEL WITH YOUR BABY

If you are taking your little one overseas, refer to this list to make sure you are fully prepared:

1. Passport - Your child needs one to travel internationally, no matter how young.

2. Visas - If you are an American citizen, you get a free pass into most places, but you still need to check up on visas. If you are not a citizen of your country of residence, make sure your child is able to re-enter once you leave.

3. Language - While it's really fun to be adventurous in non-English speaking countries, it might not be such a great idea while you are just getting into the parenting thing. At least ensure that you know how to say basic words like "taxi", "doctor" and "bathroom" in the local language.

4. Vaccinations - Before you embark on exotic travels, check with your doctor about recommended vaccinations for that area. Some may not be available for babies.

5. Epidemics - Avoid all places that have been used in the same sentence as "SARS", "H1N1" or any other serious epidemic.

6. Availability of products - While you can stock up before you leave, camping in the Amazon with your baby is not a good idea if you don't have access to basic supplies like medicines and clean water.

7. Foods (particularly if you have special dietary needs) can be tricky in some countries. Carry jar foods or get accommodation with a kitchenette so you can cook baby's meals.

8. Political stability: This may sound a bit dramatic, but in today's day and age, it is important to assess the political stability of a country before planning a trip there with your child. While nothing gets you more familiar with a country than using its emergency services, it is not a situation you want to be in with a new baby.

LIST #FORTY-SEVEN:
THE COMPLETE PACKING LIST FOR THE FIRST TRIP WITH YOUR BABY

This list will vary depending on how long you are going for, if you are staying in a hotel, service apartment or home, and the age of your child. For the most part though, these are things you will need to consider when packing for your first trip.

1. Clothes - Consider the weather and carry extras of everything: t-shirts, vests, sweaters, pants, jackets, raincoat, night suits, socks and hats.

2. Blankets -One for the pram/flight and one for the crib.

3. Medicines - Refer to **LIST #SIX**.

4. Toiletries - Body wash, shampoo, lotion, diaper rash cream, nappies, wipes, diaper disposal bags, towel and face napkin.

5. Portability - Travel pram, baby carrier and portacot if you have one.

6. Eating - Breasts if breastfeeding! Formula, bottles, sterilizer. If on solids: hand blender, bowls, spoons, sponge, dishwashing soap and disposable bibs.

7. Pacifier(s).

8. Toys - Avoid bulky toys that take up space and weight. Carry plastic bath books, which are lighter and much tougher to destroy.

PARENTING

LIST #FORTY-EIGHT:
THE 12 BIGGEST MYTHS ABOUT PARENTHOOD

Don't' let anyone tell you otherwise…

1. "The newborn stage is easy - all they do is eat, sleep, and poop!"
   This is true but it takes at least 3 months for you as parents and the baby to get into a groove. Plus throw in colic, reflux, sleep-deprivation and breastfeeding issues and you're practically asking for a refund!

2. "The newborn stage is the hardest – once they start communicating, it's a piece of cake".
   No, because by then it's their own opinions and needs that they are communicating and until they are about 5, they refuse to understand that the world does not revolve around them.

3. "You will fall in love with your child the instant that you lay eyes on them".
   Bonding time is important and can actually take time, especially for dads. This is completely normal so don't get worried if it doesn't feel completely natural on day 1. You just met, after all!

4. "You will instinctively know what to do in all situations".
   First time parenting is hard and it is normal that you will not know what to do in all situations. Seek advice where you feel unsure and don't be afraid to ask. Being a new parent is hard for everyone and chances are if your child is going through it, another child has been through it already. Try to learn from other people's experiences.

5. "You baby can sleep through the night after the first couple of weeks if you follow a certain routine".
   Any parent that tells you that their child is consistently sleeping through the night after the first few weeks and has done so ever since birth is LYING!!!!

6. "It gets easier after the first 6 months".
   Unfortunately this is not entirely true. Whilst you will hopefully be getting more sleep after the first 6 months, you baby will also be sleeping less during the day, which means less down time for you as a

parent. It does mean though that your baby will engage with you a lot more which makes parenting all the more rewarding.

7. "Becoming a parent will bring you closer as a couple".
This is true, but be warned that so is the opposite. Having a child can highlight major differences in your upbringing and value systems and the sleep deprivation and lack of control can put a real strain on your relationship. Make sure to communicate your needs and to LISTEN to each other to avoid irreparable damage.

8. "Your parents will be able to tell you everything you need to know".
At a high level, yes, but things have changed since your parents had kids and they tend to forget a lot of the basics, like how to set a routine and deal with a colicky child.

9. "If I do anything that makes my child angry or sad, he won't love me".
Wrong. Children have extremely short-term memories and will easily forgive and forget. If you are acting in your child's best interest, believe that they will be better off for it, not worse.

10. "You need to have good parents to be good parents".
Sometimes the best parents are those who have learned from the mistakes of their own. Think back to your own childhood and try to extract the best things from it. And if you can't find anything, wipe your slate clean and start from scratch.

11. "There are good babies, and bad babies".
There is no such thing. Babies are babies, and they all have good days and bad ones. You can be grateful for having a child that is not as difficult as other ones, but never forget that all babies go through alternating states of angel and demon. It is not indicative of how they will be as adults although your response to them might be.

12. "Breastfeeding is a fool-proof contraceptive".
Nope. You can get pregnant while breastfeeding, so unless you want Irish twins, make sure you use protection.

LIST #FORTY-NINE:
13 REASONS BEING A NEW PARENT SUCKS

Nobody tells you how hard it is, and by the time you find out, it's too late to give them back!

1. It will probably be about 15 years before your next sleep-in.

2. When you leave the house for 2 hours you have to pack like you are leaving for two weeks (and two weeks is like two months, and so on).

3. Holidays (if they ever happen) are more work and not in any way restful. In fact, they are a mere change of scene.

4. You are the one responsible for changing the diapers, especially the ones classified as a "poo-nami". Definition: a poo which explodes out the sides of the diaper and up the back of your child requiring a complete change of clothes and possibly a bath for all involved.

5. You may never have a night of uninterrupted sleep again.

6. Going out for a night out becomes a logistical nightmare. Babies have a sixth sense and become instantly unsettled when you are late for the ballet.

7. A simple night of dinner and a movie will now cost a lot more (factoring in the price of a babysitter).

8. You will lose some friends who don't have kids!

9. Everybody thinks that they are the expert on how to raise your child and will constantly bombard you with endless and unsolicited advice.

10. You are expected to host anybody who wants to come over and see your new baby at any time and without warning. And yes, they will expect coffee and cake with the baby viewing.

11. You won't get to eat any more meals with your partner as one of you will be feeding your child, changing their diaper, or putting her to sleep.

12. One shoulder will always be covered in your child's vomit. This is especially true when you are about to leave for work in the morning and on your most expensive item of clothing.

13. You find yourself in a race with other new parents to have the child that teethes, walks and talks the fastest.

LIST #FIFTY:
14 REASONS BEING A PARENT IS THE MOST PHENOMENAL THING IN THE WORLD

Why it's all worth it...

1. You will develop a love for your child greater than anything else in the world. Other people will try and prepare you for this feeling, but until you experience it first hand, you will not understand.

2. The first time your child smiles at you is the most amazing feeling ever. This will most likely happen after the first couple of months of your baby being born and usually coincides with when you are feeling most exhausted. That's Mother Nature for you!

3. You will constantly be filled with pride at everything your child does, no matter how repetitive or average!

4. No matter what your baby looks like, you will truly believe she is the most beautiful child ever and not be able to understand why you are not stopped on the street by people telling you this.

5. Watching your child develop into a full person is the most rewarding and satisfying experience ever.

6. In no time, your offspring will act like you, talk like you and want to be just like you. Till they turn thirteen, anyway.

7. If you are single, babies are the biggest chick-magnet.

8. You make all the rules. Although everyone will try and tell you how to raise your child, ultimately you make the final call.

9. You will receive the most amazing hugs and kisses from your child at random moments.

10. For the first 10 years of your child's life, they will think you are the most perfect person in the world.

11. Parenthood elevates you to "adult" status in society - people suddenly think you know what you are doing and treat you accordingly.

12. You get to cut the lines in airports, grocery stores, and for buses!

13. Babies are at their happiest in the mornings, which reminds you to appreciate each new day.

14. You now have a legacy to leave behind in this world.

BONUS LISTS

1. **FOUR EFFECTIVE WAYS TO BURP YOUR BABY**

1. Sometimes when your baby feeds, they swallow air as well. This can cause discomfort and your baby will need to be burped. Once of the easiest methods to burp your baby is to place him/her on your shoulder and gently pat her back. It will take a few minutes for the burp and subsequent relief.

2. Place him over your lap on his stomach. Gently pat your baby's back and this should relieve him/her of any air that may be trapped due to feeding.

3. Many people swear by the method of laying your baby on her back and bending her legs and gently guiding them towards her chest. This can sometime push any air that may be trapped inside her body out.

4. For a newborn (3 months and under), hold the baby under the chin to stretch his back to dislodge any gas bubbles.

7 STEPS TO SUCCESSFUL BREASTFEEDING

1. Start as early as possible: ideally in the first half to two hours after birth, but certainly within the first twelve hours.

2. Make sure an experienced midwife teaches your partner how to attach your baby to the breast properly from the beginning.

3. Demand feed the baby right from the start.

4. Feed the baby for as long as he wants to at every feed - within reason. If the feeds are taking longer than 30 minutes for a few days after the milk has come in, perhaps he's not attached well or his positioning is wrong so he finds it difficult to swallow.

5. If her nipples are sore, it just means something needs adjusting: either the baby's attachment to the breast or his position. It's not that he's sucking too long or that he's sucking too vigorously.

6. Don't miss the night feeds. It's likely that they boost your milk supply more than daytime feeds. Feeding is also tranquillizing, and may help the baby sleep better.

7. Her nipples produce substances that attract the baby and help him attach to the breast, so don't use creams, lotions, potions or that magic ointment that the old lady round the corner says will stop nipple soreness.

8. If your baby keeps falling asleep on the boob, make him less comfortable by removing a layer of clothing or tickling his feet.

Made in the USA
Middletown, DE
16 December 2019